Seasons
of
Change

Anne B Say

DEDICATION

This book is dedicated to my families. My parents and my sister have passed away, which leaves my ties to my big brother. Bless his heart, he gets all my love. Rick Bostick, you are the best big brother a girl could have. My husband, Terry, has been my greatest encourager and proofreader. With his support this book and the places it takes me moved from dreams to reality. Most importantly, this is dedicated to my heavenly Father, who wrote my story long before I was born, and who allows me the grace to share it.

This is also dedicated to the people in my life who became family. The leader, Mr. Jon Bohm, who took me under his wing to help me find my way; Mrs. Brandi Kochian, my best friend, who never gives up on me, and my "big sisters" at Riverstone Church, Mrs. Biddie Steed, Mrs. Gini Crisp, and Mrs. Julie Smith, who love and care for me so unconditionally.

It is of paramount importance to acknowledge the following group of incredible women who dedicated hours to piloting some of the assignments in this book. Their encouragement and feedback fueled me to finish well. I love and adore each one of you.

Mrs. Brandi Kochian
Mrs. Jan Priddy
Mrs. Donna Hyder
Ms. Rhonda Fleming
Ms. Nicola Say
Mrs. Charlene Payne
Ms. Amy Epperly
Ms. Kassie Bohanon
Mrs. Opal Bush
Ms. Patti Gordon

and special thanks to Mrs. Theresa Harvard Johnson, whose encouragement, prayers, and vision is a gift to all who know her.

CONTENTS

Preface

The title for this book came to me in the early 2000's. If you've never experienced something "coming to you", it's kind of like receiving something you didn't ask for. Instead of a tangible gift, it's more like the answer to a question you didn't ask.

Sometimes things come to you which you didn't ask for. Sometimes things are offered and you reach out and take them. And sometimes you want something so badly that you're willing to roll up your sleeves and do whatever it takes to get it. That's my story. Some things came to me, a few were offered, but what I value the most is the stuff I was willing to work for.

Freedom came from that effort. I wanted change so badly that I sought it out. For too long I had watched people who were free. I sat through talks given by people who lived in a place I wanted to be. Finally, someone came into my life who was willing to give me the time and who help me find the path. For that person and that time, I am deeply grateful.

Seasons of Change is a process of going through seasons of growth. The changing seasons which I experienced brought me freedom. They helped me love myself, love my story, and love others for who they are. The purpose of this journal is to help others experience their freedom also. While each person's story is unique, and the need for breakthrough in any area varies from person to person, the general principals of freedom are universal. My hope and prayer is that you will find yours here, that you will find the journal activities thought provoking, healing, and ultimately the seasons of change will bring you freedom in areas that will bring you an increase in joy, peace, relationships, and that you will change the world where you leave your imprint.

I believe certain core values shaped this book:

- People were created to be free, physically, emotionally, and spiritually.
- Freedom has been misunderstood and that misunderstanding has kept people enslaved.
- A journey can bring breakthrough to freedom from a variety of entrapments.
- Symbolic acts can be a powerful release.
- Freedom can be contagious. My breakthrough can be your breakthrough.

How to use this journal

This is an interactive, creative journal. Seasons of Change parallels the seasons of the year. Each season has entries that correspond to natural manifestations of that season. For example, Spring includes concepts such as "cleaning", "planting", "creation".

The entries for each season include 4 focus points:

- **Theme**
- **Look**
- **Explore**
- **Respond**

Theme provides a focus point for the entry. There may be more than one entry for a particular theme.

Look builds the landscape for the theme. It may tell a story, explain a concept, or paint a picture.

Explore invites you to think, pray, dream, remember as you look at the landscape.

Respond encourages you to engage in your thoughts, prayers, dreams, and memories providing a foundation for healing and wholeness. The respond portion is an opportunity to artistically create a visual of the landscape as you see it through redemptive eyes.

The length of time you choose to stay here is flexible. Some journal entries may be completed in a day, some may last for several days as you process more intimate topics. You may find it helpful to return back to a particular journal entry weeks later as you continue the process.

The journal pages are provided, and you are encouraged to compile your responses as you desire.

Helpful tools to keep on hand:

- A binder or art journal
- Colored pens, pencils, doodling pens
- Paints
- Magazines, scissors, glue
- Fabric, trims, sequins, etc.

WEEK I
THEME: COMMUNICATION

<u>Look:</u>

The way we communicate with others and with ourselves ultimately determines the quality of our lives. Tony Robbins

We sat in my new doctor's office and listened as he went over the blood work. Brilliantly, almost gracefully, he moved around the two pages of acronyms and numbers. He talked as if we were in his thoughts rather than in his office. "When I see this... it makes me wonder about..." Occasionally he would glance over to my husband and I and smile. I could tell he truly enjoyed his work. It was as if he were putting together a puzzle, and slowly the picture was emerging.

We've been working on my thyroid function. Half of it is working great; the other half, not so much.

"Your adrenals." he said. "Can't talk thyroid without looking at your adrenal glands." We sat and listened to his sentences and half-sentences. He flipped back and forth between the pages. Smiling more and chattering about anatomy and body systems. I am fascinated, maybe because 40 years ago I slept through my 10th grade biology class with slow-speaking Mr. Graham.

Finally the doctor looked at us. "Your pituitary gland is in a heightened state of alert." He explained more, but basically said that the communication from my pituitary to my hormone glands, all of them, is all crazy excited. My thyroid is confused, my adrenals are all excited. It probably isn't helping my menopause either, I thought.

There is only one organ that talks to the pituitary; the

hypothalamus. "Let's focus our attention there for a while and see if everything else levels out a bit." There is always a root; a place where it all begins.

Explore:

The hypothalamus sets off a communication channel to the pituitary, which then signals the hormonal organs. In my case the hypothalamus was yelling at the pituitary, which then began screaming at my thyroid, adrenals, and ovaries. One bad initial signal set off a chain reaction. It all began at the root, the hypothalamus.

There is a root for our communication also. It begins in the heart. Our own communication works the same way. It begins in the heart, and goes through the mind and forms a thought. From the thought our attitudes and actions form. Whatever the condition of our heart toward someone or something, it will come out in our communication with people, both verbal and non-verbal. It comes out in our attitude and our actions.

In the gospel of Luke, Jesus calls it fruit. He describes it in the following metaphor.

You'll never find choice fruit hanging on a bad, unhealthy tree. And rotten fruit doesn't hang on a good, healthy tree. Every tree will be revealed by the quality of the fruit it produces. Figs or grapes will never be picked off of thorn trees. People are known in this same way. Out of the virtue stored in their hearts, good and upright people will produce good fruit. But out of the evil hidden in their hearts, evil ones will produce what is evil. For the overflow of what has been stored in your heart will be seen by your fruit and will be heard in your words. Luke 6:43-45 Passion Translation.

It all begins in the heart. Sometimes it might not have anything to do with the "receiver" of the communication. The hypothalamus was edgy because of something inside it. So it lashed out.

Our communication is very much like that. Eventually whatever has been brewing in our heart will come out at the slightest annoyance. It may be someone who has cut you off on the road; someone doesn't hold the door for you and it bangs back in to your side; or maybe it's the 500th time you asked that child to stop tapping his pencil like that.

Why is it important to get to the root? Think about your heart, both physically and emotionally. Physically, your heart keeps you alive. It keeps the blood flowing throughout your vital organs and to all parts of your body. It is your life organ. If your heart isn't working properly, your body becomes unable to function optimally, and you become vulnerable for even more disease and illness.

Emotionally, your heart is the same. If you are not emotionally healthy, it will leave you vulnerable for other negatives to affect your health. Medical science has understood for years that most of our physical ailments have roots in our emotional health. Stress is attributed to at least 85% of our health challenges. Your emotional health is as vital to your life as your physical health.

It all comes from the inside out. Proverbs 4:23 reminds us that out of our heart flows the wellspring of life. Is your well spring contaminated? Whatever is at the root, the great news is there is always hope.

My doctor wasn't discouraged about the results of my bloodwork. He was ready, willing, and able to offer the solution. When we become aware of a sour root in our heart, God is ready, willing, and able to help clean it up. All you have to do is ask.

Respond:

When your communication is malfunctioning, it will affect your relationships, your work, your success in life, and your levels of peace, joy, and happiness. In the same way our endocrine system triggers a chain reaction, our communication can do the same thing, whether it is positive or negative. We all want peace. We all want to be successful, and certainly most of us want good relationships.

This week ask God to help you take a closer examination at your thoughts. Make a list of your thoughts over the week. The good, the bad, and the ugly. Look for patterns. What title could you give some of the patterns? As I walked through this process the first time, I noticed repeated phrases such as, "I resent that..." That root I labeled "resentment". Even today, over 10 years later, I guard against resentment. When words and phrases like that appear in my thoughts, I pay attention. The wellspring of my life is about to be contaminated, and I need to stop it before it goes any further.

As you see patterns in your thoughts, the next step is to follow them to the root. Asking yourself two questions can help get to the root.

1. *What am I feeling/thinking?*
2. *Why am I feeling/thinking that way?*

When I looked to the root of "resentment" thoughts, I often found an "expectation". My expectations had been unmet, and I had taken offense. Someone may be speaking disrespectfully, or ignoring, or not praising my work. Whatever the situation, my reaction was often rooted in an expectation. When we place expectations on others we set ourselves up for disappointment. We set ourselves up for a trajectory of negative emotions and unhealthy responses.

Once the heart of your thoughts have labels, you can make choices to have a different thought. If you have placed an expectation on someone or something the solution is often more simple than we realize. Once you have identified the unhealthy root, instead of leaving it there, pluck it out and replace it with a different thought. Give yourself a break, and give yourself a better, healthier starting point.

If you are having a hard time finding a better thought toward that person or situation, you have excellent resources to draw from.

1. Go back to an affirmation you have written, about yourself, or about your life.
2. Go back to something God might have already spoken to you.
3. Ask Him for a new, healthy thought. Ask Him what He thinks about the situation.

When resentment pops up in my thoughts, I remember a scripture that God gave me a long while back about how He sees me. I remember that I am the salt of the earth. Matthew 5:13. It is one of the scriptural affirmations I have for myself. It replaces the negative with something positive. Even if it has little to do with the current circumstance. It's a better starting place for a new thought.

So, make your thought lists this week. Ask God to help you. He is faithful.

Behold, I will do a new thing, Now it shall spring forth; Shall you not know it? I will even make a road in the wilderness and rivers in the desert. Isaiah 43:19 (ASV)

JOURNAL PAGE

JOURNAL PAGE

WEEK 2
THEME: RELATIONSHIPS

<u>Look:</u>

Jesus, therefore, six days before the Passover, came to Bethany where Lazarus was, whom Jesus had raised from the dead. So they made Him a supper there, and Martha was serving; but Lazarus was one of those reclining at the table with Him. Mary then took a pound of very costly perfume of pure nard, and anointed the feet of Jesus and wiped His feet with her hair; and the house was filled with the fragrance of the perfume. John 12:1-4 (NIV)

Three siblings, a small family unit, yet each of them has a different role in this story. Martha, as she is often described, is serving. She apparently knows how to handle a large, hungry crowd. She serves, at times to extreme, but she serves. If she didn't, people might not eat. Lazarus has recently been raised from the dead. Surely he was hungry; surely he had some questions for Jesus. So Lazarus sits, reclining with Jesus at the table, where Martha was serving everyone. He's asking, listening, learning, just being. Mary worships expressively; she pours expensive perfume on the feet of Jesus. Mary is often described as being at the feet of Jesus. It's where she connects with Him, loves Him, and learns from Him.

There are so many variables which impact our communication, and so many more when our communication involves intimate family members. Values, personality patterns, mental processing differences, and especially attitudes that have formed from wounds our hearts have received.

In my family we were a melting pot of types and styles. My father valued critical thinking, so a good conversation involved playing "devil's advocate" and encouraging debate that looked more like a verbal World War than a critical thinking exercise. He didn't do it to be mean; he did it because of what he valued.

People communicate differently. We communicate love differently. We communicate disappointment and frustration differently. We communicate rejection, coping, and insecurities differently. Things that some of us value, others don't, or at least not as much. To add to the layers of differences, we have different needs at different times in our lives, and we communicate those differently also.

Explore:

When people live in community, whether at home, at work, or socially, their uniqueness begins to surface. People have different ways of relating, expressing thoughts, desires, and ideas, in general simply communicating.

How mundane life would be if we were all the same! Yet we are drawn to those like us. We spend time in groups with those with whom we have common interests, or jobs, or styles. Our very nature allows us to easily define people by their work or interests, their opinions, backgrounds, even dreams and desires. We tend to draw boundaries and exclude those who are unlike us.

Consider your family, your friends, and your co-workers. God is a creative God. Each person is fearfully and wonderfully made. The uniqueness of each individual is a product of their story. How they express themselves, what they hold valuable, and the dreams of their heart.

The Lord God made each of us uniquely. We are a people with freedom to choose what we like and dislike, what we value, and what we dream. Never the less we live in a broken world. Life in a broken world makes it easy to suffer wounds and hurts. As people with wounds and hurts we bump up against other people with wounds and hurts. This is the environment where we are challenged to love out of our own lives into other's, despite our differences. This is where we learn to love the person, despite the attitudes and actions. The example with Lazarus, Martha, and Mary is our model to follow. God always give us opportunity to grow deeper into the likeness of Jesus. He will bring those people into your life until you learn to love well.

Respond:

Lazarus, Martha, and Mary were siblings, but they had significant value differences, especially the women. Yet Jesus loved and valued each one of them for who they were. He valued each one with their unique needs, hurts, and hang-ups. You are valued just as much, just as you are today. So are the people in your life who bump up against your needs, hurts, and hang-ups.

Who are the people in your life? Identify them. Take the week and make a complete list. Work on it each day. Think about who they are. Describe your relationship with them. What is the foundation of your relationship? Is your relationship based on familial ties? Business? Common interests? Take your time and consider who they are.

Represent them creatively. Group them how you wish, but be as creative as you can with the process.

Our goal here is to pay attention to the differences in those around you. Try to build value and appreciation for who they are and what they do. To be able to love all of them, the good and the bad.

Can you acknowledge, accept and appreciate them for who they are? Or do you judge them for what they do and how they believe? Are you fully present in the conversations or rushed and distracted? Are you seeking to understand their point of view, or express your own as a counter opinion? Can you validate people even when they disagree with you and challenge what you value?

People are different, but each one has value. Strive to find the value in everyone.

Pick one person and choose to make application in that relationship. Imagine considering what it is like to be that person? What would it be like to walk in their shoes? Commit first to understand them, instead of judging, or walking away. It's a process that may make your relationships richer and more rewarding. It is surely a process of learning how to love well.

This scripture text is true for you. It is also true for everyone on your list.

> *For you formed my innermost being;*
> *Shaping my delicate "inside"*
> *And my intricate "outside",*
> *And wove them all together in my mother's womb.*
> *I thank you, God, for making me so mysteriously complex!*
> *Everything you do is marvelously breathtaking.*
> *It simply amazes me to think about it!*
> *How thoroughly you know me, Lord!*
> *You even formed every bone in my body*
> *When you created me in the secret place;*
> *Carefully, skillfully shaping me*
> *From nothing to something*
> *You saw who You created me to be*
> *Before I became me!*
> *Before I'd even seen the light of day,*
> *The number of days You'd planned for me*
> *Were already recorded in your book.*
> Psalm 139:13-16 (The Passion Translation)

JOURNAL PAGE

JOURNAL PAGE

WEEK 3
THEME: CREATING

Look:

Creativity is intelligence having fun. Albert Einstein

My husband and I enjoy camping. Occasionally we will pack up for a couple of days mid-week and head to a nearby lake. One trip was especially memorable. It couldn't be more perfect; the weather, the venue, and the fact that no one else was around. It's exactly what we needed. Exactly what I needed.

Since we are surrounded by the beauty of nature, my husband began a conversation about how God is a creator God. We talked about 3 aspects of Him as Creator.

1st. Our minds went to all the things He has created which we enjoy so much and so in this moment: lakes and trees, birds (we saw the most spectacularly colored bird yesterday), the sounds of nature like the wind, cicadas, water lapping on the shore. We even remarked about the bullfrogs in our back yard at home. God has created so much, simply for us to enjoy.

God is a Father God, and He has a father's heart toward us. Our earthly fathers' hearts are designed to mirror many aspects of our Heavenly Father's heart. Our earthly fathers, along with our earthly mothers, prepare a home, provide the opportunity for education, teach and comfort us as we grow and mature. In the same way our earthly fathers create a home and environment in which we can grow and thrive, our Heavenly Father has done the same. It's a very exciting parallel when you begin to explore this wildly diverse planet we call home.

Any loving father wants his child to enjoy the home he has created.

My granddaughter loves to explore the drawers and cabinets, and purses and bags around my daughter's home. It thrills her parents as she peeks and pokes around. They take pleasure in her delight as she discovers new things and how they work. If a loving father finds that much joy in his child, how much more so does our Heavenly father? Does it thrill His heart when we see a spectacularly blue bird land in our campsite?

2nd. Creator God enjoys creating with His children. Many fathers enjoy building things with their kids; tree houses, barns, crafts, model cars and airplanes, even cookies, pancakes and waffles. A loving father finds honor and love in creating alongside his children. He enjoys sharing the discovery, sharing the satisfaction of work.

Father God is much the same way. When we have dreams and plans for our lives, He works alongside us, guiding our thoughts and the work of our hands. The plans for careers, homes, family, and vacations, all come with a Father who longs to work with us to see our hearts desires fulfilled.

My step-daughter is a chef. I am more than certain that Father God creates with her. I can see the pleasure on her face, and I can feel the pleasure in Father's. My oldest daughter creates environments. She sees the clients goal and creates incredibly engaging, unique, and powerful environments. She thrives on creating the challenge of the process.

There are many scripture verses about how our souls were designed to be creative.

Delight yourself in the LORD; And He will give you the desires of your heart. Psalm 37:4 (NAS)

May He grant you your heart's desire and fulfill all your counsel! Psalm 20:4 (NAS)

3rd. What if… As we talked about all these parallels in the Father's heart, my mind wondered about the deeper dreams in our hearts. Too many of us have dead dreams, dreams that have died from disappointment; Dreams that have been buried in the catacombs of our hearts, long forgotten and rarely remembered. Our earthly fathers would come quickly if we began talking about our dreams. Our earthly fathers' hearts were made to hear the dreams of our hearts.

He fulfills the desire of those who fear him; he also hears their cry and saves them. Psalm 145:19 (NAS)

A few years back I began searching my heart for dead dreams. How far back would I have to go? Did I even have any? Were they dead and buried, or had they never been born? In my opinion we all have dreams. They are there by our nature. Our spirit and soul were created to contain dreams, therefore we surely had them at some point in our lives.

My own father died when I was young. I am certain he would have cared about my dreams. He would have loved to hear about them. He would have wanted to equip me to fulfill them. It would have honored him to know my heart and help me fulfill them, even if they weren't His dreams for me. He would have wanted to see *my* dreams fulfilled.

Explore:

What if Father God created us to dream? What if His Father heart found honor and joy in knowing what our dreams are? Would you go find them and bring them to Him? Would you unearth those tombstones and dig them up like a buried treasure lost then found?

Spend some time thinking about your buried dreams. Listen deeply, not just to your thoughts. Give yourself time to review your life. Consider the treasure map. Things might not be easily discernable at first, but as you familiarize yourself with the map, you might begin to see things in a new light. Look at the landscape, look at the obvious and the not so obvious. Try to look at the familiar with a sense of newness. Sometimes we name and judge something before we truly know what we are looking at.

Respond:

1st. Consider the things that feed your soul like nothing else. List all the things that bring you joy. Add artwork, words, and pictures, anything that might relate to the items on your list.

When your joy list and artwork is complete add it to your binder.

2nd. List the things you've sought after and achieved in your life. Make a thankful list for the resources and people who have helped you achieve them.

When your thankful list is complete, consider writing a thank you note to one of the people who has helped. It can be short and simple, or elaborate and lengthy. Allow yourself the opportunity to express the gratitude and acknowledge the person.

3rd. What if Father God created us to dream? What if His Father heart found honor and joy in knowing what our dreams are? Would you go find them and bring them to Him? Would you unearth those tombstones and dig them up like a buried treasure lost then found?

Were you able to find a buried dream? Sometimes this is as difficult as trying to read that treasure map and find a supposed buried treasure. Don't give up! Even if it seems a silly dream, dig it up. Look at it a while. Maybe allow yourself to grieve it, but definitely allow yourself to consider resurrecting it. Resurrecting a dream may mean looking at it in a new way.

Allow yourself to breathe life into that old dream and see what might grow from it. Make your artwork and add it to your binder.

JOURNAL PAGE

JOURNAL PAGE

WEEK 4
THEME: KNOTS, part 1

Look:

She was the most beautiful, complicated thing I'd ever seen. A tangled mess of silky string. And all I wanted of life, was to sit down cross-legged and untie her knots. Atticus

It seemed like I had been untangling the knot for hours. It also seemed like I wasn't making any progress. I could feel the angst of impatience welling up inside of me.

Knots form in almost anything. Necklaces, rope, yarn. How does that happen? It is put down, left untouched, but when it's picked up there's a big knot. This particular day it was yarn. Yarn is the one that doesn't make any sense at all. The yarn manufacturers sell it in that funky "skein" shape. The first thing the knitter does is make it into a ball. Why don't they just sell it in a ball? To make a ball from a "skein" you begin by pulling the appendage out from the inside. For some mysterious reason balling with the outside end of the yarn never works. So, more times than not the appendage works into a knot during the balling process. Maybe it's just me, but it happens.

A second way yarn gets tangles is while unknitting (taking it out) in order to redo, or try a different pattern. Suddenly, poof! There's a knot.

This one particular morning I sat unknotting in order to use the yarn for a different project. It took hours and felt like days, to work the knot out of this huge mess. The temptation to grab the scissors, cut the knotted mess, and call it done was overwhelming. The challenge for a group of us was to use up these small balls of yarn making as many scarves as possible. We gave them to homeless people. Wasting that much yarn wasn't going to work.

Cutting the yarn would only compromise the finished piece. Cutting the yarn means the strength of the weave is weakened. Picking at the yarn through the knotted strands, I thought about the nice scarf that would come from this mess. It'll be the same yarn that is presently unusable and unattractive, but the potential beauty was only hinted at by the color and texture.

The angst inside of me to cut this knot out felt very similar to the angst in another area of my life. Sometime earlier I had asked God to help me heal from some things. It had been a long season as God revealed and healed places I'd kept deep down inside me.

As my fingers picked through the layers of the knot and balled up the yarn, God began to speak into my heart. He gently showed me how similar I am to the yarn. As much as I wanted to hasten the process, this would only compromise the integrity of the finished work He is doing inside of me. Such vision and hope were placed in me that day. It helped me surrender to His process of untying my knots.

Knots do not become untangled by themselves. Left alone, the knots tangle up. They have to be untangled by someone. There is a Someone who is ready, willing, and able to untangle our knots.

Explore:

Knots can appear in so many different kinds of objects in our lives. Some things can be knotted and still function. Christmas tree lights, extension cords, headphones and earbuds, computer cords can all be knotted and still function. They might not look good, but they are still functional. Some things can be knotted and both lose their ability to function and look pretty bad. Water ski rope, yarn, necklaces, and garden hoses won't work when they're knotted up.

Knots can have fascinating names. After researching names of knots, I grouped them into categories I made up.

This week have some fun with the names of knots. We will dig deeper next week. For now, simply create.

You might tell a story about one of knots. You might write a story about how the knot got its name. You could draw a picture of the knot, research the knot and make it with rope, or sculpt it out of clay.

Respond:

This week let your creativity flow. We will pick up more personal work next week. This week, simply create.

National knots

- Dutch marine bowline
- Englishman's knot
- European death knot
- Flemish bend
- Italian hitch
- Portuguese bowline (aka French bowline)

Cultural knots

- Beer knot
- Corned beef knot
- Highwayman's hitch
- Farmer's loop
- Zeppelin bend (aka jam-proof)

Regional knots

- Eskimo bowline
- Icicle hitch
- Packer's knot

- Falconer's knot
- Yosemite bowline

Just plain mean knots

- Strangle knot
- Thief knot

Personalized knots

- Ashley's stopper knot
- Blake's hitch
- Jack Ketch's knot
- Matthew Walker's knot
- Rosendahl bend
- Poldo tackle

Animal knots

- Cat's paw
- Dogshank

Strange and Bizarre knots

- Common whipping
- Portuguese whipping
- West country whipping
- Handcuff knot

Emotionally unhealthy knots:

- Adjustable bend
- Adjustable loop
- Monkey's fist
- Power cinch
- Grief knot (aka what knot)

JOURNAL PAGE

JOURNAL PAGE

WEEK 5
THEME: KNOTS, part 2

Look:

"I wish the king had never come to me. I wish none of this had happened". ~Frodo

"So do all who live to see such times, but that is not for them to decide. All we have to decide is what to do with the time that is given to us". ~Gandalf

This week we will look more closely at some types of knots. We will consider what they might look like in people.

Knots are formed because of lies. Untangling the knots is the process of moving from false beliefs (lies) to the truth. It's the process of moving from a lie to the truth. The knotted yarn is a mess. The yarn is pretty, but it's not able to be all that it could be because of the knots.

The challenges of life are a lot like untying a knot. Years ago I was in a season of challenges. They were mountains in my path and I was desperately trying to move mountains. As I discovered these principles, I discovered valuable keys to this mountain-moving process. To this day they are my main strategy when any challenge crosses my path.

I had made many attempts on my own to get "breakthrough". One day, after I realized how exhausted I was, I asked God what the knots in my life were. What I've learned since that day is that God is ready, willing, and able to answer those kinds of questions. When we are in Christ, we have the Holy Spirit living inside of us. The Holy Spirit knows exactly where the knots are and exactly how they got there.

The Holy Spirit helps us in our weakness. For example, we don't know what God wants us to pray for. But the Holy Spirit prays for us with groanings that cannot be expressed in words. Romans 8:26

As God began to reveal to me the knotted areas in my life, there was not a smudge of condemnation. He was showing me the truth about myself. Then He showed me the truth in Christ. The truth is where we live in freedom. Jesus tells us it is all about being free.

If you abide in My word, then you are truly disciples of Mine, and you shall know the truth, and the truth shall make you free. John 8:31-32 (NAS)

When we live with knots, ie. lies, or false beliefs, we are not only restrained from living, we are actually dying. It can feel like a slow suffocation.

This can be pictured this way: A lie is a false belief. Our beliefs direct our thoughts. Our thoughts determine our actions. When we are knotted up with false beliefs, we act in such a way as to move us further away from the source of our life, which is Christ. "Thought is action in rehearsal." *Author Unknown*

Yarn left all to itself will only get more knotted. It won't go away. In the same manner, false beliefs (lies) do not go away on their own. It is a law of nature.

My knots had decades of time to grow and get stronger. They had grown deep in my belief system. They were foundational. Being able to separate the lies from the truth, to untie the knots, and let the truth become my belief system was life changing for me.

Explore:

The first thing God did was to name my knots. My biggest knots came from a short list of needs. Naming things is a powerful place to begin to heal and grow. My knots' names were resentfulness, abandonment, unloved, and judgement. Those knots developed into belief systems. My beliefs became: I have to protect myself to be safe. I have to fend for myself because no one else will. I am unloved (especially if I fail). I am right. These beliefs dictated my actions. Because I usually felt unsafe, I often "ran" when there were perceived threats. Because my voice had been silenced by my wounded heart, I often felt resentful toward others. This in turn built walls up around my heart and added to the abandonment feelings. It was all a vicious cycle, fueled by my responses, and leaving me in more and more emotional pain.

Our beliefs direct our thoughts. Our thoughts direct our actions. Our actions determine our direction and destination in life. Whether we live free, or slowly die without knowing how to live. If I didn't get my knots untied, I knew I would die.

Respond:

Ask God where the knots are in your life. Listen to your repeated thought patterns for clues. Do you hear repeated phrases such as, "I resent that..." or "She should(n't)..." or "I hate...". These kinds of phrases will give you good clues to your knot names.

Ask God to help you name them. As you put names on your knots, let your creativity flow. Draw them, create them, or explain what they look like in your mind's eye.

Journal through your thoughts. Let yourself be honest with yourself. Remember,

There is now therefore no condemnation for those who are in Christ. Romans 8:1 (NAS)

God will always draw you toward healing and wholeness. He will never draw you into condemnation.

We will go a bit further next week. For now, create your names for your knots. Allow yourself the gift of finding and untying the knots. Sometimes we have to get real in order to get better. Yes, you may cry at the memories, at the mistakes, but crying helps purge out the negative from our souls. We won't stay here, but we are wise to walk through this. Let's do it together.

JOURNAL PAGE

.

JOURNAL PAGE

WEEK 6
THEME: KNOTS, part 3

Look:

Dear God,

Please untie the knots that are in my mind, my heart, and my life. Remove the have nots, cannots, and the do nots. Erase the will nots, may nots, might nots that may find a home in my heart. Release me from the could nots, would nots, and should nots that obstruct my life. And most of all, dear God, I ask that you remove from my mind, my heart, and my lie all of the "am nots" that I have allowed to hold me back. Especially the thought that I am not good enough. Amen. Author Unknown

Since our knots are created from lies we've believed, we can ask the question, where did the lie come from? As human beings created in the image of a wonderful, holy God, we have a short list of basic needs. Each one of us has a body, soul (mind, will, and emotions), and a spirit. We all, at the core level, need certain things to satisfy our triune beings. Our task here is to focus on our soul, the mind, will and emotions. Our list of needs includes security, significance, acceptance, satisfaction, honesty, and the need to connect spiritually.

Remember the tangled mess of yarn I was trying to get unknotted so that I could use it? This is a perfect picture of partnering with God to untangle our knots so that we can become more useful, more beautiful, more of what we are created to be. During this season of surrender, I spent many hours, days and months working to cooperate with God to untie these knots. It meant the difference between life and death for me. I knew there was a better life and I desperately wanted it. The good news is that God desperately wanted to give it to me. He desperately wants to give it to you, too.

Explore:

My knots had names. Now came the untangling. This is the "God did" part. Mark Sanborn writes in "Up, Down, or Sideways", We don't lack for knowing; we lack for doing." Let's put more doing in our lives.

I knew that God was working in me. I wanted to cooperate, but I had never done anything like this before. The one thing I did do was show up every day to get more from Him.

I "set my mind" on a course of letting God show me my knots and show me how to let Him untie them. In other words, I was mindful of the truth, what was actually happening. I didn't condemn myself for the ugly character flaws. There was no condemnation, only healing happening. However, it wasn't always easy to keep my mind set. This particular season seemed to last forever. In retrospect, it was more like being homeschooled and not knowing how to do it.

Many days it was a battle to keep my mind set. The bible tells us there is a liar, one who hates us with a fierce passion. The liar uses our disappointments and wounds to our hearts to help us believe lies. This liar wants nothing more than to keep us in knots. When we are exploring our knots and where they came from we need to remember to keep our mind set in the truth. God is partnering with us to get the knots out. He is committed to setting us free. He knows the joy, peace, and exciting life that awaits us. It was focusing on that lifesaving goal that kept me alive.

Your mind was not designed to be empty of thoughts. You will always be thinking about something. The beautiful fact is that you can choose what to think about.

Romans chapter 8 teaches us that the mind set on the Spirit is life and peace. Our mindset is the will to follow or obey the dominant interest of the mind. Our mind produces thoughts that become healthy cells. These thoughts help our emotions and then our actions (our will) follow suit. To follow after the Spirit of God in us means we conform our thoughts to what we know is true and resist things that we know will take us away from that. In other words, our "yes" is bigger than our "no". We persevere because we know and trust the promised outcome.

We will have some time later to create healthy statements to keep in our minds when we need a replacement thought. For now, let's continue with our knot untying.

I was working intently on untangling the yarn. God was working intently on helping me untangle my soul knots. Resisting the urge to cut the knot helped me persevere in allowing God to show me the lies I had believed so that they could get untangled. Once the first knots became untangled the process became easy, and my "yes" became bigger. Those first knots untangled were my first fruits of what was to come, what I could become as I walked in freedom.

We all need to be encouraged as we go along. Consider making encouragement markers somewhere in your creative process. Use them in those seasons when not much seems to be happening. They will remind you of how far you've come, and they will be fuel for your spirit and soul to keep going.

Our part is showing up. Every day. Our part is to show up and have time with Him, allowing His Spirit to intercede for us. God knows our heart's desire is to heal. His Spirit intercedes for us, and as always, it is according to the will of our Father.

As God unties the knots He does so much more, beyond what we hope and dream. He never takes away a negative without replacing it with a positive. He heals us; He heals relationships; He opens doors for love to flow; He gives us opportunities we have longed for, but were not ready for until now.

Respond:

God has shown you some knots. You know their names. Now it's time to get them untangled.

1. Call them by name. Then stop agreeing with them. This can begin as a moment by moment process, but as the days and weeks go on it will become something more to be aware of as it occurs less and less often. This is part of the "showing up" every day. Keeping your mindset in the truth will help you get stronger. Persevere! It is not impossible!

When God named my "resentfulness" knot. I began asking Him why I felt resentful. I quickly understood that I had placed expectations on people. The expectations were in my heart and head, but never did I utter a request to anyone. When He named my "abandonment" knot, He also showed me where that began. In the same manner as untying a knotted yarn, I quickly got to the central issue and moved in to some serious untying.

2. Forgive those who've offended you and caused you to believe the lie. Forgiveness is a vital process for a couple of reasons. One reason is that when we have unforgiveness in our hearts we are essentially sitting in judgement of the offender(s) and their actions. We want to see punishment and be paid retribution. The reality is there is only One who has the right to sit in that Judgement seat. It is God's place, not ours to judge. Forgiveness moves us out of the way so that the One who judges can work with our offender(s). Another reason it is important to forgive is because unforgiveness keeps us in misery, not necessarily the others. It frees us to get on with our lives without dragging around this dead weight we were never designed to carry. Finally, we forgive because we have been forgiven.

Forgiveness doesn't mean we become a doormat for people to continue abusing us. It may mean setting healthier boundaries, creating a larger space between us and others until we are stronger in our own soul and spirit.

At this point it might be helpful to reach out for some support in the untangling process. Forgiveness and boundaries are important issues and it is helpful to seek out wise council in these areas.

3. Replace the lies and the woundings with the truth. God is always interested in giving us an upgrade. Redemption means coming out of the old and stepping into the new. Our minds will always contain a thought. This step is the practice of choosing what thoughts to allow in your mind.

Replacing the negative thoughts (or lies) may not come easily. The easiest way is to ask God what the truth is. My rule of thumb for listening to His answer is to grab the very first thing that comes across my mind. It may be a word, a picture, a song, etc. Whatever He answers, that is a piece of truth for you. If you want more information, ask Him what it means.

This truth is for you to use to replace the lie. When that knotted thought comes back into your head, call it out. Call it a lie and state the truth. This breaks the power of the lie, and moves your thoughts to truth, peace, joy, and guards your heart against the unforgiveness that might try to latch on again.

When I hear my self-talk begin uttering things like, "She should've…" I check in with Jesus. I take that thought to Him. I ask Him where it came from. Then I ask for forgiveness for judging, for placing expectations, for whatever He points to that needs to be addressed. Now here's the important part. I give Him that thought, and I ask Him for a new one. Whatever thought I receive it will be good because He only gives good things. Then I keep that new thought guarded in my head so that the old one doesn't come back.

Understanding where the lie occurred and forgiving those involved, and moving your thoughts to truthful places is part of "showing up". It may happen many times the first day, but shortly you will find yourself going days walking in the truth.

Show up. Show up every day. Tend to your mind daily. Watch your thoughts and control them so that they don't control you. This is the process of untying knots and keeping them untied.

Here are some of my motivating verses that keep me persevering.

It was for freedom that Christ set us free; therefore, keep standing firm and do not be subject again to a yoke of slavery. Galatians 5:1

But in all these things we overwhelmingly conquer through Him who loved us. Romans 8:37 (NAS)

JOURNAL PAGE

JOURNAL PAGE

WEEK 7
THEME: PLANTING

Look:

Don't judge each day by the harvest you reap but by the seeds that you plant. Robert Louis Stevenson

There are days when you simply don't have a clue what will happen. My husband likes to call it the surprise of Serendipity. Serendipity, he says, favors the prepared spirit. If we stay open, and expect something to happen, we will be better prepared to receive it when it comes.

One morning recently I received two encouraging words. The first came written in a text. The second came verbally through a woman I greatly respect and admire.

The law of sowing and reaping is more real than we might care to admit. It's not often that you can sow and reap in the same day. It can happen, but it's not the norm. Like planting a garden from seed, growing things to harvest takes time. Often the better quality stuff takes much longer to grow. Stuff that comes quickly tends to be "cheap". It doesn't "cost" us much in terms of patience.

We are such an impatient people. We seem to have lost our ability to wait for it. If the line is too long, we won't bother. If we can't get overnight shipping, we won't order it. Sometimes we are willing to pay more just to have it now. The phrase "time is money" might actually mean something different than how we use it. Hummm….

So, this particular morning these two ladies sowed kind, encouraging words into my day, into my life. It totally changed the flavor of my morning. It lifted my spirits and helped me to do a little kind encouraging sowing into others' lives as I went on with my own day. Their words were unsolicited, from their heart toward me, and they each took the minute to communicate them to me. I felt abundantly blessed. They spoke words to me that came from over a year of meeting with them, both in group settings, and they happened to want to share with me that particular day.

Their words changed my attitude that morning. Their words touched my heart in such a way that left me wanting, even looking, for someone else I might encourage. Sowing these words into me allowed me to sow into others. It's the law of sowing and reaping.

In the spring time I like to plan and plant my vegetable garden. I particularly enjoy starting my plants from seeds. My favorites include tomatoes, kale, beans, spaghetti squash, garlic, and sweet potatoes. They won't be ready for harvest for a couple months. I'll have to sow now though if I want to enjoy them later. During the summer as we enjoy the tomatoes I'll remember the days when I planted the seeds. I'll remember taking great care of them as they sprouted and grew, gradually getting strong enough to put outside.

Kindness and encouragement are the same as these seeds. So often we sow a kind word, many times over and over, until one day weeks and months in the future, it comes back to us. It's the law of sowing and reaping. This law works for pretty much everything, good, bad, and ugly. Ugly words and actions also work by sowing and reaping.

I try to weigh my words before I speak them. Please note, I said "try". Not only do I passionately desire everyone to get free and be all they are created to be, I also want to sow good things for my future self. I try to make sure my heart is in a good place toward each person. (see Relationships)

Explore:

What have you got currently growing in your life? Often we rarely pay attention until we see the harvest. Have you got some bad stuff growing in one or two of your relationships? Look back over time. Most likely you planted something that grew into this unhealthy thing. Be aware of what kinds of seeds you are sowing today. More than likely it will come back to you in the future. Make it count for the better. It truly does matter what we sow and reap.

As children of God, He wants us to make a difference in this world. Jesus tasked us with the joy of expanding His Father's kingdom here on earth. We do that by planting the fruit of the Spirit, by being good stewards of what He has given us.

Listen to this! Behold, the sower went out to sow; as he was sowing, some seed fell beside the road, and the birds came and ate it up. "Other seed fell on the rocky ground where it did not have much soil; and immediately it sprang up because it had no depth of soil." And after the sun had risen, it was scorched; and because it had no root, it withered away. "Other seed fell among the thorns, and the thorns came up and choked it, and it yielded no crop." Other seeds fell into the good soil, and as they grew up and increased, they yielded a crop and produced thirty, sixty, and a hundredfold. Mark 4:3-8 (NAS)

Do not be deceived, God is not mocked; for whatever a man sows, this he will also reap. Galatians 6:7 (NAS)

The wicked earns deceptive wages, But he who sows righteousness gets a true reward. Proverbs 11:18 (NAS)

According to what I have seen, those who plow iniquity And those who sow trouble harvest it. Job 4:8 (NAS)

Respond:

1. What are you currently experiencing in your day, week, month, or even year?

2. Consider all types of relationships: family, professional, social.

3. How would you describe some of your relationships? Can you put names under some of the following categories? Consider them to be trees. Draw them as such. Put the names underneath them such as:

Kind   Patient   Loving   Faithful   Joyous   Gentle   Honest

Disrespectful   Untrusting   Offensive   Misunderstood
Resentful   Judgmental

4. How do you turn this around? If you want different fruit, you must plant a different tree.

Choose just one situation, just one relationship in which to plant a different tree. Choose one that is not too far down a negative path. Ask yourself some questions:

- What am I feeling here?
- Why am I feeling this way?
- When was the first time I felt this way?
- What need wasn't met?

Be honest and realistic. Take some time to forgive them. (go back to the Knots if you need to) Not to make what they did okay, but forgive them for not being what you needed in the moment.

If you want different outcomes, the process begins with planting different beginnings. It has to include planting a different tree. You can't plant an apple tree and expect to grow grapes. If you want grapes, you have to plant a grape vine.

It also has to include patience. Some things take longer to grow to maturity than others. Are you willing to be patient? Are you willing to gently nurture that little seed you just planted, or are you expecting it to be able to survive a tornado right after it sprouted up?

What is it going to take to grow that seed? You know you want that awesome harvest so what are you willing to do to make that new seed grow?

How do you turn resentfulness into mercy and acceptance?

How do you turn disrespect into appreciation?

Take some time to consider what is currently growing. What would you like to see? Make a plan to plant that new tree. Be bold and daring!

Now, let's plant a new tree. Let's dig up the old one, and plant something new.

Label the old tree.

Now create your new tree.

Let your creative juices flow!

JOURNAL PAGE

JOURNAL PAGE

WEEK 8
THEME: CIRCUMSTANCES

Look:

Character, not circumstance, makes the person. Booker T. Washington

The sun is always shining. Whether the clouds get in the way or not, the sun is always shining. Sometime things obscure it, but that never changes the fact that it is a constant source of light, heat, and life.

The sun can be:

- Blocked by trees or clouds
- Cooled by the wind
- Dampened by the rain or snow
- Forgotten or unnoticed by tornados, tsunamis, and earthquakes

But it is always shinning. It is always itself because it doesn't let the weather change it. Is the sun ever freaked out by the storm? It just keeps shining.

Sometimes there are things that obscure us from living from our identity. Circumstances can become distracting and even overwhelming. When we respond to our circumstances out of anything other than our identity we can easily get derailed from our peace, prosperity, and productivity.

If you were the sun, you would always remain being the sun. You wouldn't be discouraged when clouds get in the way, or when storms come and block you completely. You would simply continue being yourself.

The sun brings light, warmth, and life to our world. There are things each of us bring to our worlds also. I am gifted as an encourager and a teacher. People often reach out to me to listen, to help shed new light on circumstances in their lives, and to be a safe place to just be themselves.

Unfortunately, when things get in my way I am likely to stop being an encourager and start behaving more like a destroyer. My identity can become derailed when people talk about me wrongly, either to my face or behind my back. It's like the clouds and trees, it only has a short, minimal impact. When there is tension and discord in my family it disrupts the level of peace and quiet in my life. These "storms" may last a while. In the north, the snow storms can last for a few days. Sometimes I have life circumstances which feel a lot like a tornado or hurricane. When these come they steal my joy and leave me discouraged, and unproductive. Divorce, abusive relationships, and losing my parents were big storms in my life.

It would be helpful on most days to not let the trees and clouds obscure my identity. I would much rather be a person who is constant despite the wind, rain, and snow. These "lesser" weather conditions are a detriment to my character when I respond to them from something other than who I am.

Explore:

The solution might be easier than we think. It really is a matter of focus. We respond to our circumstances when we have unmet needs. We stop being ourselves and begin reacting. Any unmet need can cause us to respond from an unhealthy place. Being grounded in our identity will help keep us strong and consistent in our actions and reactions.

Unmet needs can come under a sense of acceptance and belonging, the need for love, the need to feel satisfied and successful at our work, and even the need to be spiritual. We are triune beings, so our needs can be physical, emotional, or spiritual. They can create casual and occasional challenges, like trees and clouds occasionally block the sun. They can create more significant impact, like wind that leaves the sunlight, but takes away the warmth.

Respond:

The first response to this is to know who you are. Spend some time this week and answer the following:

1. What things in my life feed my soul like nothing else?

2. What things in my life am I really good at?

If you have a hard time with these questions, ask 3 people how they would answer them about you. Make sure they are people who will tell you the truth, not just what they think you want to hear. It's important to know who you are in order to understand when you aren't behaving from your identity. Tools such as the DISC or the Myers-Briggs can help.

If you are really struggling with this, email me at anne@annebsay.com and we can work through a couple of exercises via email.

3. What are the trees and clouds in your life? What is blocking, but not constantly obscuring you?

4. Are there any storms to which you are responding?

5. Are you in a longer season where you are not pursuing your dreams or goals at all?

Use your creativity to express the clouds, storms, and earthquakes in your life, past or present. Begin to identify areas where you are responding instead of remaining constant in who you are. We will come back to more of this later, so simply begin the process of being aware.

JOURNAL PAGE

JOURNAL PAGE

WEEK 9
THEME: CREATING SPACE

Look:

Most of us spend too much time on what is urgent and not enough time on what is important. Stephen R. Covey

You can't fit a square peg into a round hole. Neither can you fill up space which is already full.

full: *adjective*, fuller, fullest.

1. completely filled; containing all that can be held.
2. complete; entire; maximum.
3. of the maximum size, amount, extent, volume, etc.

It's a matter of size. It's a matter of mass. It's one of those laws of nature that is simply inflexible.

We are much like that as people. Our bodies can only hold so much. Remember the last time you ate too much? Full; Stuffed; About to burst. Our souls (mind, will, and emotions) are much like that also. Our minds can only focus on one, maybe two things at a time. There's only enough active mental space to effectively concentrate. Think about your will. Even for the soul that "wants it all", there is still a limited space. The wanting it all doesn't work. Will involves choice, and many things are mutually exclusive. The ever-powerful emotions are the heavy lifters in capacity. This is the place where space is deeply significant. Emotions occupy space. If there is something occupying our emotions, it will have to be removed in order for something else to take its place. Two things cannot occupy the same place at the same time. It's simply a matter of size and mass.

Everyone carries their share of "baggage"; wounds and lies we pick up from living in a broken world. It is as much a fact of nature as gravity, taxes, or death.

Some of us try to manage on our own, accepting it as part of our lot, "just the way I am". The problem is, when we are all loaded down with our luggage, we are left unable to carry anything else, even if it's something good, something valuable.

People who carry all this baggage throughout their whole life are often labeled "strong". "They can handle a lot."

This is generally true, they *are* strong and *can* handle a lot. Let's ask a different question. What are they unable to handle because they are? Are they carrying the best things?

Explore:

In my own journey, I carried the baggage of a strong woman. Even after I became aware of what I was carrying, I dressed it up and labeled it "a complete set of designer baggage". It was an attempt to use humor to mask my junk. Maybe in a sense I was proud of what I was carrying. I was independent, capable of doing a lot, sometimes all at one time. Looking back, it feels more like I sacrificed intimacy for efficiency. I was able to carry a lot, but it wasn't without consequences.

There were a lot of things I wasn't able to do. Many of them were important. As a single mom I thought I should be both mom and dad. I thought I had to carry a double load, carry the responsibilities of both parents. Because of that mindset there were many things I couldn't do.

When we carry too much we are limited from what we can do. We are limited because we can't do much else but carry our baggage.

- We can't hug someone who really needs a hug.
- We can't hold the hand of a child.

- We can't cook a decent meal for a friend or neighbor, build a project for fun or function, nor can we just sit and enjoy a good book.

How do we work through this process of creating space? Let's begin with a bird's eye view of things.

My categories look like this:

- personal time – which includes bible study, prayer, exercise, time for personal growth reading
- chores – I don't do well with clutter; that includes dirty dishes and countertops, unmade beds, and clothes left around
- work – which includes writing, video blogging, speaking, sharing oils
- ministry – this includes our weekly serving, leading a mid-week study group, and monthly visits to a local assisted living home
- social – this is important because we all need our down time with our friends. It keeps us grounded, maintains our sense of humor, and keeps us connected with each other
- family – just because the nest is empty, doesn't mean they're gone.

How do we begin to let go of some of the things we carry, in order to be free to do some other things? The next step is to prioritize the categories and the items in each category.

Here's my prioritized list:

- personal time – priority: non-negotiable. This is daily time, and my preference is mornings, minimum 2 hours to include all items.
- chores – priority: To be honest, I will pick up the living space and do the dishes, but general cleaning goes to the bottom of the list. The priority is to make sure the living spaces are picked up.

- work – priority: high. I set my hours on Sunday for the week. It's a high priority to stick to the hours. It helps me stay on track. It also keeps me from over-extending myself, and also to utilize smaller amounts of time to chip away at big projects.
- ministry – priority: high. These are scheduled commitments in my life. The hours each week are minimal, and it is both a value and a priority.
- social – priority: flexible. This is a huge area for me. Some people are re-charged by being out with friends, some are re-charged by being home and unwinding. Know thyself, as my mom would say. I am conscious of who I haven't seen in a while and who I need to see on a more regular basis. I need my alone time, and I also need my girlfriend time. My goal is to connect with a couple regularly, some often, and some occasionally.
- family – priority: high. Sometimes it's just a phone call, but I am aware of how long it's been since we've chatted.

I can give hours to these, but life happens, seasons change and so will the hours dedicated to individual items. So for now, let's just determine the priority. The point is we have to manage our time or it will get away from us and we don't get it back. If we are doing too much, we probably aren't doing some of the things we should be.

Respond:

Look at your calendar. List out the things and group them into categories. Then consider their priority. Some of the calendar items are more important than others. Work, for example, has to happen or there might not be a home to clean. Other items are there because we choose to do them. There are seasons where the priority will change, and it's important to be able to know where the give and take will occur. It may seem tedious, but it helps to have some sense of managing our time or it will get away from us.

It will help you see where you can create space.

What if we really like all these activities we do? This makes the process even more challenging.

For me the process began when I realized that I would be stepping down from youth leadership. The years I'd spent with the high school students had been so much fun. There was no rhyme or reason, it was just time. I knew it. I prayed and ask the Lord if I was sensing what He was leading. Nothing changed.

So many of us, are tied to things. I was this way for several years. As an empty-nested, single-mom, I kept a very full calendar. It kept me busy and helped to fill the void of an empty home. A lot of the events on my calendar were good things to be involved in, community service, church ministry, family time, hanging out with friends, etc. It was all good. It is all good. But at some point it became too much.

There are some principles in the bible that may help guide our thinking here.

- God created for 6 days, then He rested. Not because He was tired, but to set an example for us. Whenever a principle is laid out in scripture for the first time, it sets a precedence. God intends for us to have a rhythm in our work and rest. Genesis 1
- God will lead and guide us with His eye upon us. We have free will, but when we choose to ask Him, He promises to lead us. Psalms 32:8
- Jesus only said and only did what He saw the father do. Obviously, He asked for direction and received it. John 5:19
- Jesus rested. He got away by Himself to pray. Why do we resist resting? Jesus was God in the flesh, His God part didn't need resting, but His man part probably did.

Additionally, if He was going to hear from the Father, He probably needed to get away somewhere quiet. Mark 6:31

So, even though most of what we do with our time can be classified as "good stuff", is it all really necessary? Is it the important stuff? And most importantly, is it what God would be telling us to do in this moment?

Take the time this week to do your calendar work. Take time to listen to what God might be telling you about your schedule, your priorities.

Why is it even important? Let's look at what the Bible tell us. Here are some good, solid words to ponder.

Look carefully then how you walk, not as unwise but as wise, making the best use of the time, because the days are evil. Therefore, do not be foolish, but understand what the will of the Lord is. Ephesians 5:15-17 (NAS)

A time to love, and a time to hate; a time for war, and a time for peace. Ecclesiastes 3:8 (NAS)

Is the bible confused as to how we are to spend our time? I don't think so. I believe the bible is very clear. It does not appear to me that there is a hard and steadfast rule. Rather, Ecclesiastes 3:8 explains that there are different times and seasons. Sometimes we are called to love, at other times to stand for what we believe and know to be true. Wisdom dictates that we consider how we use our time.

For which of you, desiring to build a tower, does not first sit down and count the cost, whether he has enough to complete it? Luke 14:28 (NAS)

So teach us to number our days that we may get a heart of wisdom. Psalm 90:12 (NAS)

O Lord, make me know my end and what is the measure of my days; let me know how fleeting I am! Behold, you have made my days a few handbreadths, and my lifetime is as nothing before you. Surely all mankind stands as a mere breath! Psalm 39:4-5 (NAS)

The heart of man plans his way, but the Lord establishes his steps. Proverbs 16:9 (NAS)

JOURNAL PAGE

JOURNAL PAGE

WEEK 10
THEME: THOUGHTS

Look:

If destruction fails to entangle us, distraction will do its best. Beth Moore

When the weather is cool I like to sleep with the windows open. The crisp night air is fresh on my face, while my body is cozy and warm under the blankets. I grew up in the Adirondack Mountains this way. Toasty warm under old wool army blankets, only my face exposed to the chilly night air.

During some particularly pleasant nights I'd been opening my windows. The result was nothing resembling the refreshing, restful sleep I'd always experienced. Across the small valley from where I was living there was a small industrial plant. It was hidden down a road, tucked away from anyone passing by, and only the trucks entering and exiting gave clue to its existence, at least until I opened my windows at night.

This plant was operating a graveyard shift. At night the noise carried across the valley and into my bedroom window. The constant "beep-beep-beep" of the trucks backing up; the intermittent, ground-shaking BANG! when 2 very large somethings collided. Even the memory causes my eyes to roll to the back of my head. I needed earplugs.

Explore:

The disrupted nights continued on to disrupt my quiet time in the mornings. Each morning that week I struggled to quiet my mind, my heart, and my spirit. Engaging with the Lord became as frustrating as my job was.

For several months I was pursuing what Dallas Willard calls "conversational intimacy" with the Lord. All my life God has spoken to me through scripture, and lately He had been allowing me to hear His voice in new ways. I was learning about streams of traditions throughout church history. Richard Foster, author of "Streams of Living Water", describes them as:

1. The Prayer Filled Life
2. The Virtuous Life
3. The Spirit Empowered Life
4. The Compassionate Life
5. The Word Filled Life
6. The Sacramental Life

They are fascinating when blended all together to form a complete faith filled life. It was expanding me spiritually while not weirding me out with something cultish or crazy.

God invites us to hear Him. He invites us into a deeper, more intimate relationship.

Consider these truths:

1. God spoke to Moses face to face. Exodus 33:11
2. God awaken our ears to listen to Him. Isaiah 50:4
3. God promises to come close when we come close to Him. James 4:8
4. Jesus said we will know His voice. John 10:14-16

My heart wanted more, my faith needed more, and my head just wasn't in the game. I needed earplugs to shut out all the noise.

I journaled. *I want to hear You. Too much noise. Banging at night. Banging now in my mind. Shut it out. Quiet my heart. Relax.*

I needed spiritual earplugs. Among all the noise, all the voices clamoring in my mind for my attention, I longed to hear His soft whisper; His word for me this day.

Respond:

It is very difficult to simply empty our minds. There is always something to take up the space. The most wonderful thing I can share with you is this: You get to choose what you think about! You have control over your thoughts. This week we are going to equip you with some noise-quieting, soul-feeding, life-changing thoughts.

Here is one simple way to begin.

1. Remembering that God is alive, a real being, consider your time with Him like chatting with a close friend.
2. Play some instrumental music so there is something to listen to. See the appendix for suggestions.
3. Have a journal or some paper and pen.
4. Begin with an acknowledgement that God *does* want to have this time with you. Use the 4 truths above to craft your prayer: *Father, I thank you that you want to meet with me even more than I want to meet with you. (James 4:8) Open the ears of my heart so that I can hear you. (Isaiah 50:4) Help me to hear your voice. (John 10:14-16) Speak, for I am listening. (1 Samuel 3:10)*
5. Now ask God a simple question. Psalm 67:1 promises us that His face shines when He looks at us. Ask Him what He thinks of you right now.

One of the best tips I can share with you is to go with the absolutely, very first thought that comes to your mind. The thought that came before you even had a second to get into your own head and start thinking and questioning. Write down that word, phrase, draw the picture (even if it's not very good), note colors, smells, anything that comes with the answer.

If it's a picture, or a general word, ask Him what it means. Ask Him why He showed you or said that particular thing. Write down what He says to you. Trust yourself with the first thoughts and impressions that come across your mind.

Also, remember God always shares the good stuff. He is never condemning, critical, or ugly. So if that's what you're thinking, ask again.

If your mind wanders away here is an effective tip. Ask God about whatever your mind wandered to. Ask Him what He thinks about that thought.

Do this every day this week. Ask God a question and journal what you sense He is saying. Write them out on index cards.

Some great questions are:
1. God, what are you thinking about me right now?
2. God, tell me something fun about yourself.
3. God, what is the one thing I need to do today.
4. God, what do you want to give me for today?
5. God, who do you want me to pray for all day today?

Here is an example from my time recently. We read Psalm 67 in the Passion Translation. A phrase in the first verse particularly caught my attention. It was about God's fountain of grace. That word picture captured my attention. I picked up my journal and asked Him about the fountain of grace. Here's what I heard in my first thoughts.

Anne, you are my grace-fountain! You carry my grace with you wherever you go. Splash out!

It went on for a bit, inviting me to invite others to come, kick off their shoes, and play in the water. The water from the grace-fountain. It concluded with an invitation.

Come! Don't stand on the sidelines any longer! Come! Come enjoy the moment. Get closer so that you see my face shine on to yours.

As I sat, picturing the grace-fountain, my thoughts wandered to someone I hadn't seen for a while.

Lord, why did I suddenly think of her?

I felt in my heart that the Lord wanted me to pray for her throughout the day. So I did.

This week, have some quick, intimate conversations with your Heavenly Father. He is waiting. He loves the time with you and wants to tell you the things on His heart.

Have a great week!

JOURNAL PAGE

Anne B Say

JOURNAL PAGE

WEEK II
THEME: CLEANING

Look:

As far as the east is from the west, so far has he removed our transgressions from us. Psalm 103:12

Confession time.

I drop things. Sometimes my pen will make random line drawings on my clothing. I spill things. It happens often enough that I carry a small stain remover stick in my purse. I also have one in the kitchen drawer and one in the car. I buy a 3-pack because I go through them so quickly. It used to bother me, but now I just work around it. Thankful for my stain remover stick.

There are other areas of my life that need a stain remover. Each decade of my life has brought more spills and drops and bad mistakes. I've caused train wrecks, been caught in other people's train wrecks. I've hurt myself, and hurt others in the process. Some of those spills required a bigger stain remover. They were too big for my 3-pack.

It took a God-size, supernatural ingredient to get those stains out. It needed a heart of God made incarnate, the blood of a perfect, heaven-sent Lamb to wash my stains out.

Explore:

There are seasons of the year, and seasons of life when we might be more inclined to remember what Jesus came and accomplished through His life, His death, and His resurrection. Whatever might cause you to remember, do you find it amazing that on that cross, Jesus' shed blood covered all your sin stains? He covered yours, mine, the past ones, and the ones that haven't happened yet. With each drop He shed Jesus became the Ultimate Stain Remover.

Picture this: We are all hanging out enjoying munchies and catching up. On the tables are bowls of chips and cheese dip, tacos and salsa, chalupas and all sorts of goodies. We talk and laugh and nosh. You lean over and grab a chip, dip it in that creamy cheese dip, and a second later that cheesy goodness drips off the chip and lands on your shirt. It's there, and there is no hiding it. Out comes the stain remover stick to wash it up and set you looking fabulous again.

What are you going to do? Will you say, "No thanks. I'll just sit here looking all cheesy." That would be silly. The remedy is being handed to you, free of charge. You'll take the stain remover and go in the other room, get cleaned up, and move on. That's the purpose of a stain remover; to clean up each time there is a mess.

Jesus is so much like the stain remover. He has covered the past stains, and He has covered the ones yet to happen. Everyone has a choice what to do with this. Are you going to sit there looking cheesy and say, "No thanks."? It seems kind of silly now doesn't it. We all have stains, and we all need a Stain Remover. It's offered to everyone. Free of charge. For every stain you have.

Respond

We will always spill, drop, and make stains. Every time we will reach for the stain remover. This week, take a moment and reach for Jesus to clean up any stains that have accumulated. Free of charge.

Use your creative juices to respond how it suits you. Write, draw, paint, sculpt. Show what it looks like as your stains are removed.

Most importantly, next time you find yourself sitting looking cheesy, go clean yourself up with Jesus. He is your precious Stain

Remover.

Ponder these words this week:

And you, who were dead in your trespasses and the uncircumcision of your flesh, God made alive together with him, having forgiven us all our trespasses, by canceling the record of debt that stood against us with its legal demands. This he set aside, nailing it to the cross. He disarmed the rulers and authorities and put them to open shame, by triumphing over them in him. Colossians 2:13-15 (ESV)

He is so rich in kindness and grace that he purchased our freedom with the blood of his Son and forgave our sins. Ephesians 1:7 (NLT)

In fact, the law requires that nearly everything be cleansed with blood, and without the shedding of blood there is no forgiveness. Hebrews 9:22 (NIV)

JOURNAL PAGE

JOURNAL PAGE

WEEK 12
THEME: IDENTITY

Look:

You are God's poem. That makes you a piece of art. Art is often beautiful. More importantly, every piece of art has something of the character, vision, and values of the artist embedded within it. So it is with you. Marc Alan Schelske

Nothing has changed my life, for the better, like understanding my identity. The deeper I dig into it, the more I find.

Do you know that you have a unique, God-designed identity? Yes, you have an identity in Christ, but you are also uniquely and wonderfully made. This week we are going to explore some of our identity. We will create some "identity statements" from scripture. There are several goals of this exercise. First, to help you understand your value and worth. Second, to begin to open up your soul (your mind, will, and emotions) to who you are, uniquely. This exercise will also help you explore more scripture and move deeper into understanding your identity. You will have a foundational tool for exploring more on your own.

As a child of the Most High God, you are a princess or a prince. As a princess or prince you have at your disposal all of the resources of the King. When you entered into a relationship with Jesus, you were adopted into His royal family. All of the riches in Christ became available to you, as He chooses to dispense them.

Explore:

What resources do the following scriptures say we have?

Read each one and underline what we have been given.

Now we have received, not the spirit of the world, but the Spirit who is from God, so that we may know the things freely given to us by God. 1 Corinthians 2:12 (ESV)

For we are His workmanship, created in Christ Jesus for good works, which God prepared beforehand so that we would walk in them. Ephesians 2:10 (ESV)

Blessed be the God and Father of our Lord Jesus Christ, who has blessed us with every spiritual blessing in the heavenly places in Christ. Ephesians 1:3 (ESV)

He who believes in Me, as the Scripture said, 'From his innermost being will flow rivers of living water. John 7:38 (NAS)

For God has not given us a spirit of timidity, but of power and love and discipline. 2 Timothy 1:7 (NAS)

For God's gifts and his call are irrevocable. Romans 11:29 (NIV)

Each man has his own gift from God; one has this gift, another has that. 1 Corinthians 7:7 (NIV)

So also you, since you are zealous of spiritual gifts, seek to abound for the edification of the church. 1 Corinthians 14:12 (NAS)

Now there are varieties of gifts, but the same Spirit. 1 Corinthians 12:4 (ESV)

If you then, being evil, know how to give good gifts to your children, how much more will your Father who is in heaven give what is good to those who ask Him! Matthews 7:11 (NAS)

Did any of those stand out to you? The point here is to develop a healthy understanding of who you are. Once you're clued in to your identity, you can begin to understand your personality, your abilities, your gifts, and then be free to be that person. God created you a special way and He wants you to be what you were created to be.

People who don't know who they are, are posers. They are trying to be something they have decided is the best version of themselves. Unfortunately, to the rest of the world it is glaringly obvious they are trying to be something they aren't. This situation will leave everyone frustrated, critical and at a loss for peace and rest in our relationships.

It's better to figure out who you are and be that person. Everyone else is already taken. It's okay to be you! Your life will be better. You'll bring more glory to God.

Respond:

Let's look at a story. Bible stories are great because we get to look to see where we are, where God is, and what we might do about it.

Read John chapter 6 (NIV). Where are you in the story?

Some time after this, Jesus crossed to the far shore of the Sea of Galilee (that is, the Sea of Tiberias), and a great crowd of people followed him because they saw the signs he had performed by healing the sick. Then Jesus went up on a mountainside and sat down with his disciples. The Jewish Passover Festival was near.

When Jesus looked up and saw a great crowd coming toward him, he said to Philip, "Where shall we buy bread for these people to eat?" He asked this only to test him, for he already had in mind what he was going to do. Philip answered him, "It would take more than half a year's wages to buy enough bread for each one to have a bite!"

Another of his disciples, Andrew, Simon Peter's brother, spoke up, "Here is a boy with five small barley loaves and two small fish, but how far will they go among so many?" Jesus said, "Have the people sit down." There was plenty of grass in that place, and they sat down (about five thousand men were there). Jesus then took the loaves, gave thanks, and distributed to those who were seated as much as they wanted. He did the same with the fish.

When they had all had enough to eat, he said to his disciples, "Gather the pieces that are left over. Let nothing be wasted." So they gathered them and filled twelve baskets with the pieces of the five barley loaves left over by those who had eaten. After the people saw the sign Jesus performed, they began to say, "Surely this is the Prophet who is to come into the world." Jesus, knowing that they intended to come and make him king by force, withdrew again to a mountain by himself.

When evening came, his disciples went down to the lake, where they got into a boat and set off across the lake for Capernaum. By now it was dark, and Jesus had not yet joined them. A strong wind was blowing and the waters grew rough. When they had rowed about three or four miles, they saw Jesus approaching the boat, walking on the water; and they were frightened. But he said to them, "It is I; don't be afraid." Then they were willing to take him into the boat, and immediately the boat reached the shore where they were heading.

The next day the crowd that had stayed on the opposite shore of the lake realized that only one boat had been there, and that Jesus had not entered it with his disciples, but that they had gone away alone. Then some boats from Tiberias landed near the place where the people had eaten the bread after the Lord had given thanks. Once the crowd realized that neither Jesus nor his disciples were there, they got into the boats and went to Capernaum in search of Jesus.

When they found him on the other side of the lake, they asked him, "Rabbi, when did you get here?" Jesus answered, "Very truly I tell you, you are looking for me, not because you saw the signs I performed but because you ate the loaves and had your fill. Do not work for food that spoils, but for food that endures to eternal life, which the Son of Man will give you. For on him God the Father has placed his seal of approval."

Then they asked him, "What must we do to do the works God requires?"

Jesus answered, "The work of God is this: to believe in the one he has sent."

So they asked him, "What sign then will you give that we may see it and believe you? What will you do? Our ancestors ate the manna in the wilderness; as it is written: 'He gave them bread from heaven to eat." Jesus said to them, "Very truly I tell you, it is not Moses who has given you the bread from heaven, but it is my Father who gives you the true bread from heaven. For the bread of God is the bread that comes down from heaven and gives life to the world."

"Sir," they said, "always give us this bread." Then Jesus declared, "I am the bread of life. Whoever comes to me will never go hungry, and whoever believes in me will never be thirsty. But as I told you, you have seen me and still you do not believe. All those the Father gives me will come to me, and whoever comes to me I will never drive away. For I have come down from heaven not to do my will but to do the will of him who sent me. And this is the will of him who sent me, that I shall lose none of all those he has given me, but raise them up at the last day. For my Father's will is that everyone who looks to the Son and believes in him shall have eternal life, and I will raise them up at the last day."

At this the Jews there began to grumble about him because he said, "I am the bread that came down from heaven." They said, "Is this

*not Jesus, the son of Joseph, whose father and mother we know?
How can he now say, 'I came down from heaven'?"*

*"Stop grumbling among yourselves," Jesus answered. "No one
can come to me unless the Father who sent me draws them, and I
will raise them up at the last day. It is written in the Prophets:
'They will all be taught by God. Everyone who has heard the
Father and learned from him comes to me. No one has seen the
Father except the one who is from God; only he has seen the
Father. Very truly I tell you, the one who believes has eternal life. I
am the bread of life. Your ancestors ate the manna in the
wilderness, yet they died. But here is the bread that comes down
from heaven, which anyone may eat and not die. I am the living
bread that came down from heaven. Whoever eats this bread will
live forever. This bread is my flesh, which I will give for the life of
the world."*

*Then the Jews began to argue sharply among themselves, "How
can this man give us his flesh to eat?" Jesus said to them, "Very
truly I tell you, unless you eat the flesh of the Son of Man and drink
his blood, you have no life in you. Whoever eats my flesh and
drinks my blood has eternal life, and I will raise them up at the last
day. For my flesh is real food and my blood is real drink. Whoever
eats my flesh and drinks my blood remains in me, and I in them.
Just as the living Father sent me and I live because of the Father,
so the one who feeds on me will live because of me. This is the
bread that came down from heaven. Your ancestors ate manna and
died, but whoever feeds on this bread will live forever." He said
this while teaching in the synagogue in Capernaum.*

*On hearing it, many of his disciples said, "This is a hard teaching.
Who can accept it?" Aware that his disciples were grumbling
about this, Jesus said to them, "Does this offend you? Then what if*

you see the Son of Man ascend to where he was before! The Spirit gives life; the flesh counts for nothing. The words I have spoken to you—they are full of the Spirit and life. Yet there are some of you who do not believe." For Jesus had known from the beginning which of them did not believe and who would betray him. He went on to say, "This is why I told you that no one can come to me unless the Father has enabled them."

From this time many of his disciples turned back and no longer followed him. "You do not want to leave too, do you?" Jesus asked the Twelve. Simon Peter answered him, "Lord, to whom shall we go? You have the words of eternal life. We have come to believe and to know that you are the Holy One of God." Then Jesus replied, "Have I not chosen you, the Twelve? Yet one of you is a devil!" (He meant Judas, the son of Simon Iscariot, who, though one of the Twelve, was later to betray him.)

Now, spend the week thinking about where you are in the story. Where do you want to be? Remember, Jesus showed grace to everyone. Even Judas Iscariot.

Here are some thoughts to help guide you.

1. Philip – Walking with Jesus, but an attitude of scarcity, not understanding what's available to you
2. Andrew – Walking with Jesus, but with an attitude of possibility; Seeing potential, just not understanding the possibilities
3. The boy – if you offer it, God will use it; doesn't depend on age, financial, health, social status; everyone has something to offer;
4. in the boat – walking with Jesus daily, but not understanding who He is, what God's resources are, what His plan is? (I love the part about being willing to let Him into the boat!)

5. in the crowd at Capernaum – following just to get your needs met? Blind to the work He's done?
6. one of the Jews – not believing that Jesus really is God? Knowing the scriptures, but denying the truth?
7. one of the disciples – sugar-coating the gospel; afraid to call it what it is; afraid to turn people away;
8. Simon Peter – wouldn't go anywhere else; know Jesus is the only way

What might be preventing you from knowing/trusting/living within your identity?

Is it fear (don't believe/know God) - the disciples didn't always see either

- Review the scriptures about who your King is and what He has given you.
- Make some cards of your own; record the things He shows you.
- Ask Him when the fear first began; forgive who you need to forgive. Ask Jesus for an exchange; record what He gives you.

Is it insecurity (focusing on yourself instead of God) - there will be times of storms

- Review the scriptures about who your King is.
- Make some cards of your own; record the things He shows you.
- Ask Him to show you His tangible security.

Is it ignorance (don't know) - you only know what you know, but when you know then you can

- Consider writing some identity statements and reading them daily.

- Consider sitting in on one of my Identity workshops, either in person or online.
- Spend some time drawing, painting, sculpting, dancing to express your identity as you discover it.

Are you holding on to what you want (vs. of holding on to Him)

- Identify what you are holding onto and what it represents.
- Ask Him if it's safe to trust Him for what He wants.
- Ask Him for an exchange if you choose to give it to Jesus.

JOURNAL PAGE

JOURNAL PAGE

APPENDIX A

The following includes a sample of music for relaxing and soaking as you have your personal time.

Artists/Albums
- Steve Swanson, Hydrated

- Housefires II, Housefires

- Ben and Kelly Smith, Bread & Wine

- Julie True, Find Rest/Breathe You In

- Audrey Assad, Fortunate Fall/Heart

- Fernando Ortega, Meditations of the Heart

- Bethel Music, Without Words

ABOUT THE AUTHOR

Anne B Say's passion for encouraging others to be their best was born out of her own journey. As a single mom and special education teacher, Anne knows the challenges of balancing work and home in a pressure-filled world. Her inspirational talks share her journey to finding freedom in Christ and understanding His design for each one of us.

Anne's writings and talks create a metaphorical picture that weaves the inspiration of scripture into the realities of life. Each one integrates a powerful punch of humor, honesty, and encouragement.

Anne engages the audience in relevance and reality. Her stories encourage others to consider where they are, and with courage and hope, take a step into the life that God has planned for each one of us.

With the heart of an encourager, Anne provides practical ways for each person to embrace their journey and take the next step closer to peace, freedom, and abundant living through a closer relationship with Jesus.

Anne and her husband live in Atlanta. They enjoy their blended family and abundance of grandchildren. Anne currently writes and hosts workshops on Identity, Communication, Boundaries, and Forgiveness. You are invited to connect with her at http://www.AnneBSay.com.

Made in the USA
Monee, IL
08 March 2020